INSPIRATIONAL

Coloring Book for Teenage Girls

With Original Motivational Quotes

Thank you for choosing this coloring book

If you like this book I'd really appreciate it if you'd leave me a review and have a look at my other books.

INSPIRATIONAL
Coloring Book for Teenage Girls

With Original Motivational Quotes

© Copyright Camptys Inspirations - All rights reserved.

The content contained in this book may not be reproduced, duplicated or transmitted without direct written permission from the author or publisher. Inspirational quotes – Andrea Campbell's intellectual property

ISBN: 978-1-914997-10-5

Pocket Learner Publishing

Thank you for choosing this coloring book

If you like this book I'd really appreciate it if you'd leave me a review and have a look at my other books.

REFLECTIONS
Inspirational Coloring Journal for Women

REFLECTIONS
Inspirational Coloring Journal for Teenage Boys

REFLECTIONS
Inspirational Coloring Journal for Men

REFLECTIONS
Inspirational Coloring Journal for Adults

A range of guided and gratitude journals

A range of Activity Books

A selection of Log Books

Inspirational Coloring Book for Teenage Girls

Inspirational Coloring Book for Teenage Boys

Inspirational Coloring Book for Women

Inspirational Coloring Book for Men

Inspirational Coloring Book for Adults

Inspirational Coloring Book for Boys

Inspirational Coloring Book for Girls

Coloring book for kids aged 4-8

Coloring book for kids aged 2-4

A Gift for You

Please join our mailing list to receive periodic updates and materials. You'll also be able to keep abreast of our future publications.

As a thank you please visit the following page or scan the QR code to download a set of original inspirational posters that you can print out, frame and position in your favorite space.

http://eepurl.com/h8SU31

This coloring book belongs to:

_____

Cows don't coo,
and doves don't moo;
in all you are, say
and do,
be real, and true
to you.

Don't be surprised
if your bird
doesn't fly
if you keep it
locked in a cage.

Eagles have no business
in chicken squabbles.

If you can't do it alone,
do it together;
and if you can't go together, go it alone.

If you don't learn,
you'll be taught.

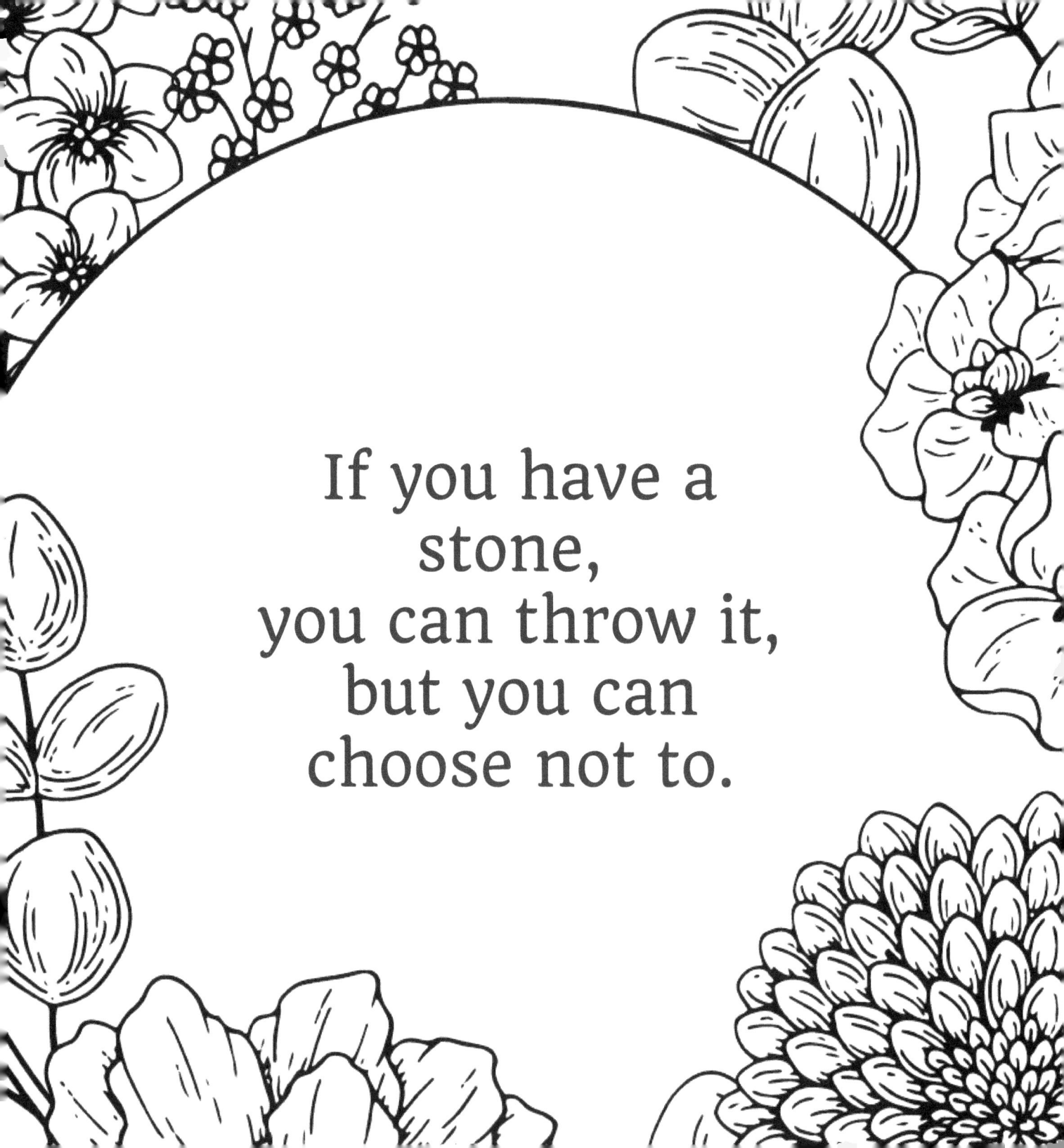

If you have a
stone,
you can throw it,
but you can
choose not to.

If you wander
too far from your
source,
you're bound to
lose your way.

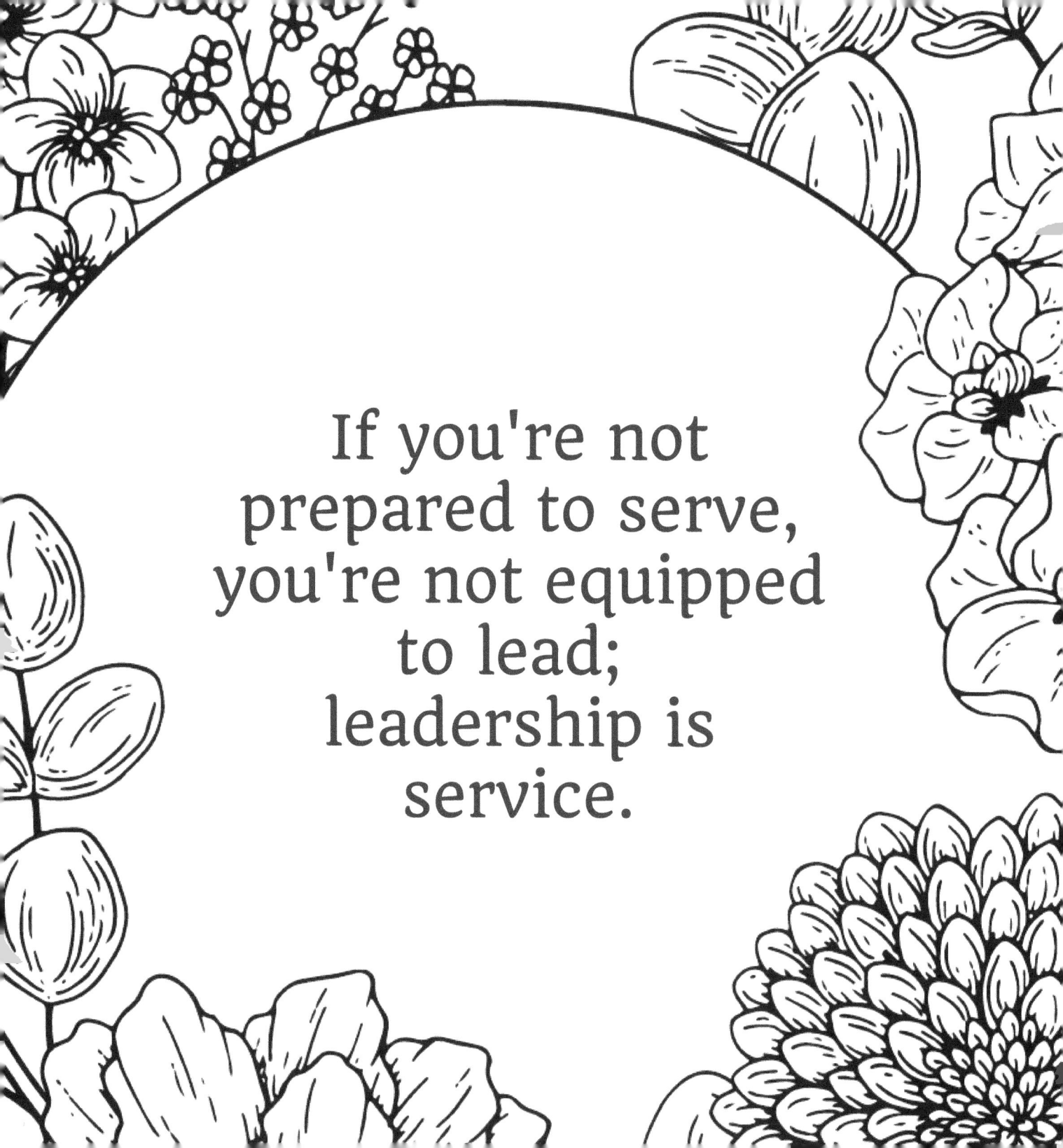

If you're not prepared to serve, you're not equipped to lead; leadership is service.

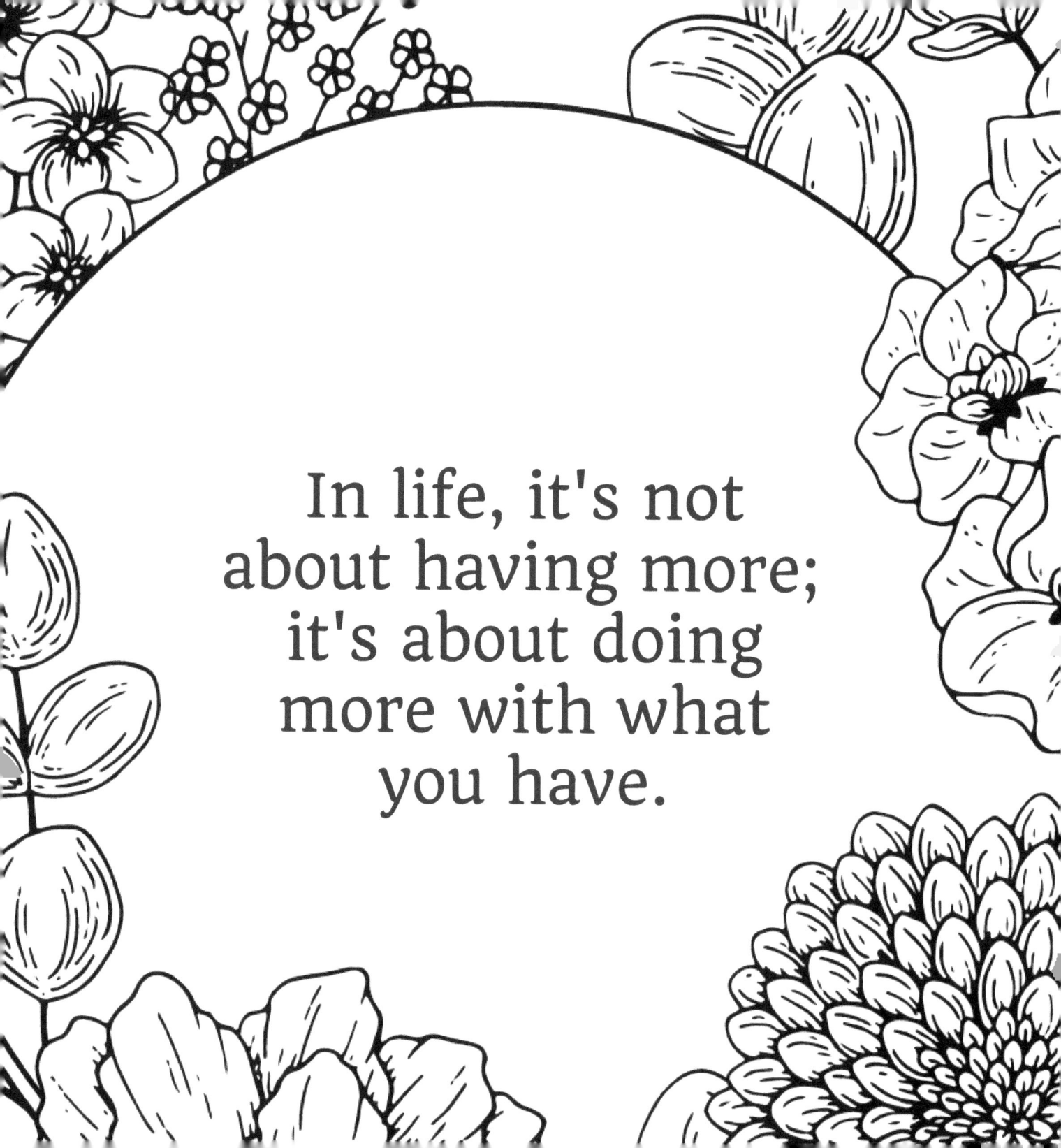

In life, it's not about having more; it's about doing more with what you have.

In order to move forward, sometimes you've got to stand still.

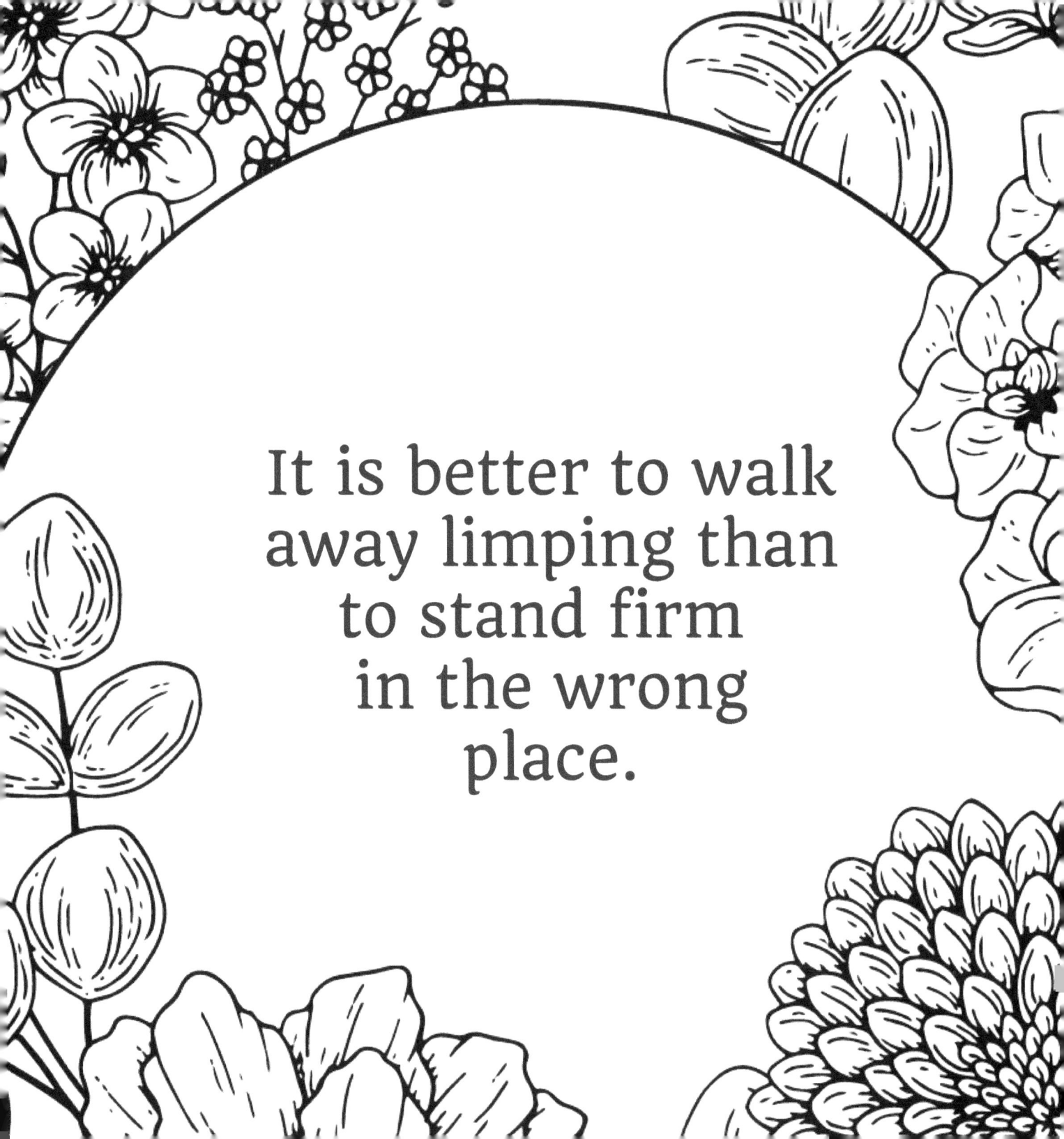

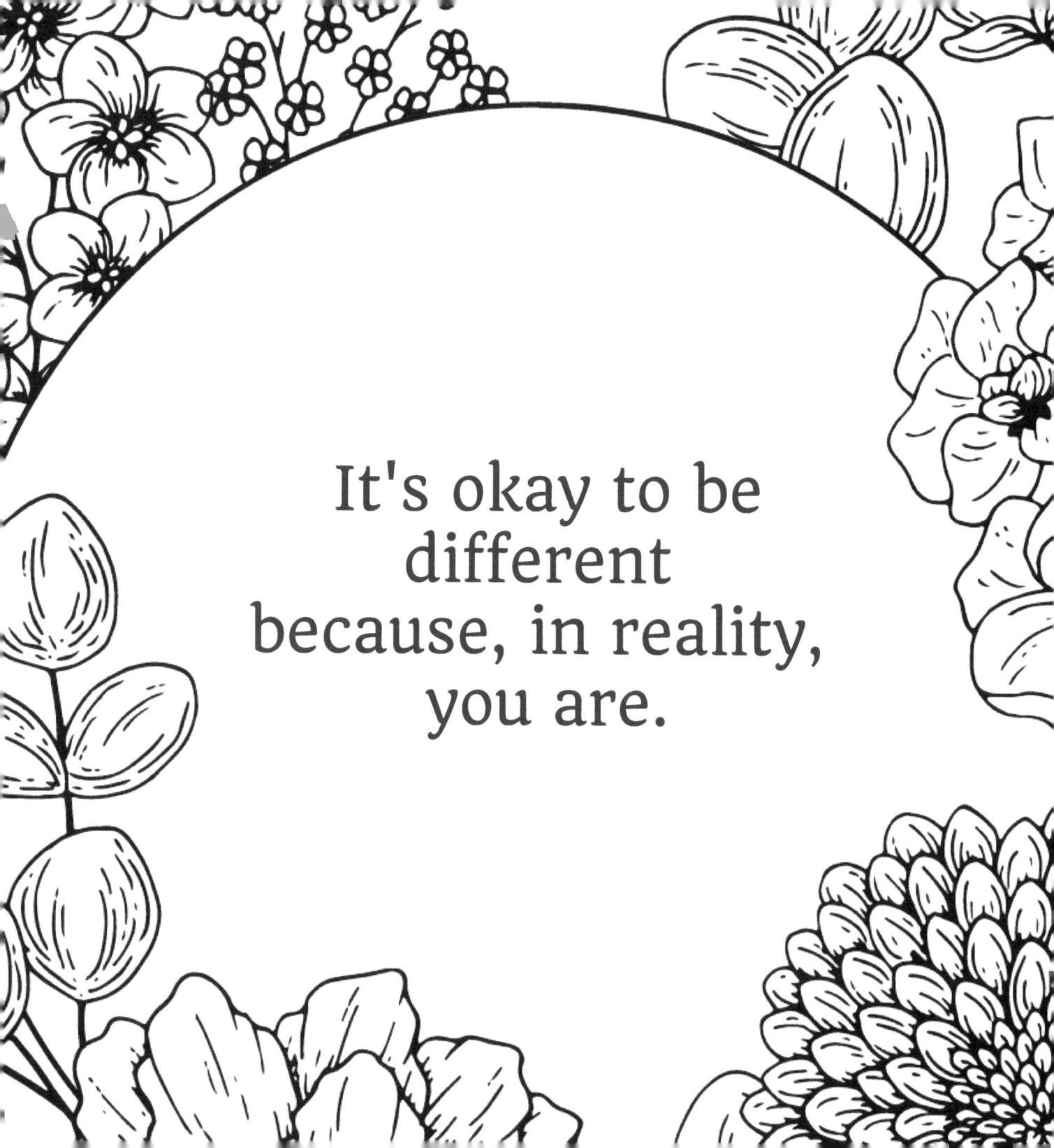

It's okay to be different because, in reality, you are.

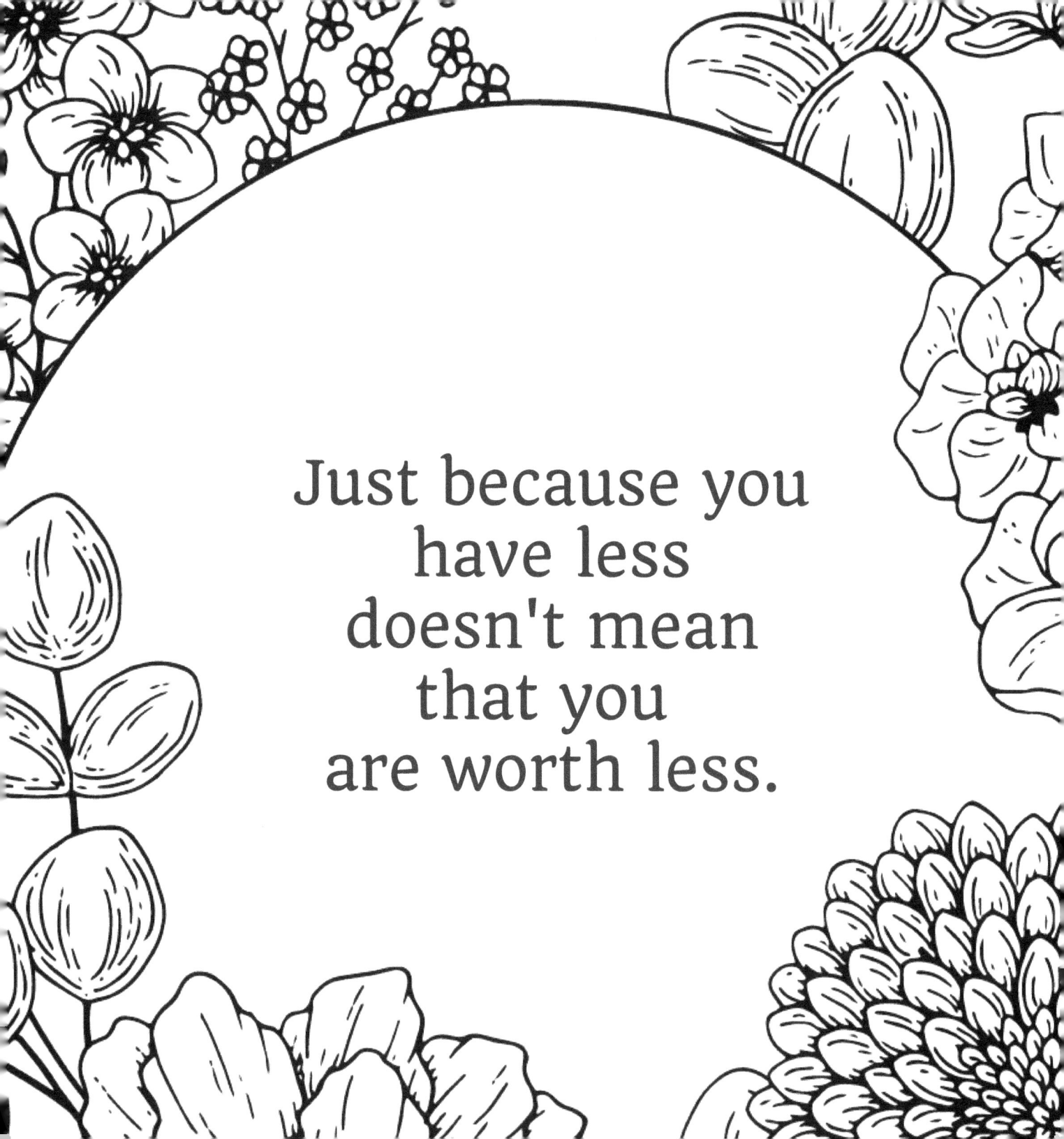
Just because you have less doesn't mean that you are worth less.

Just because your hand
can reach it
doesn't mean that
you must pick it.

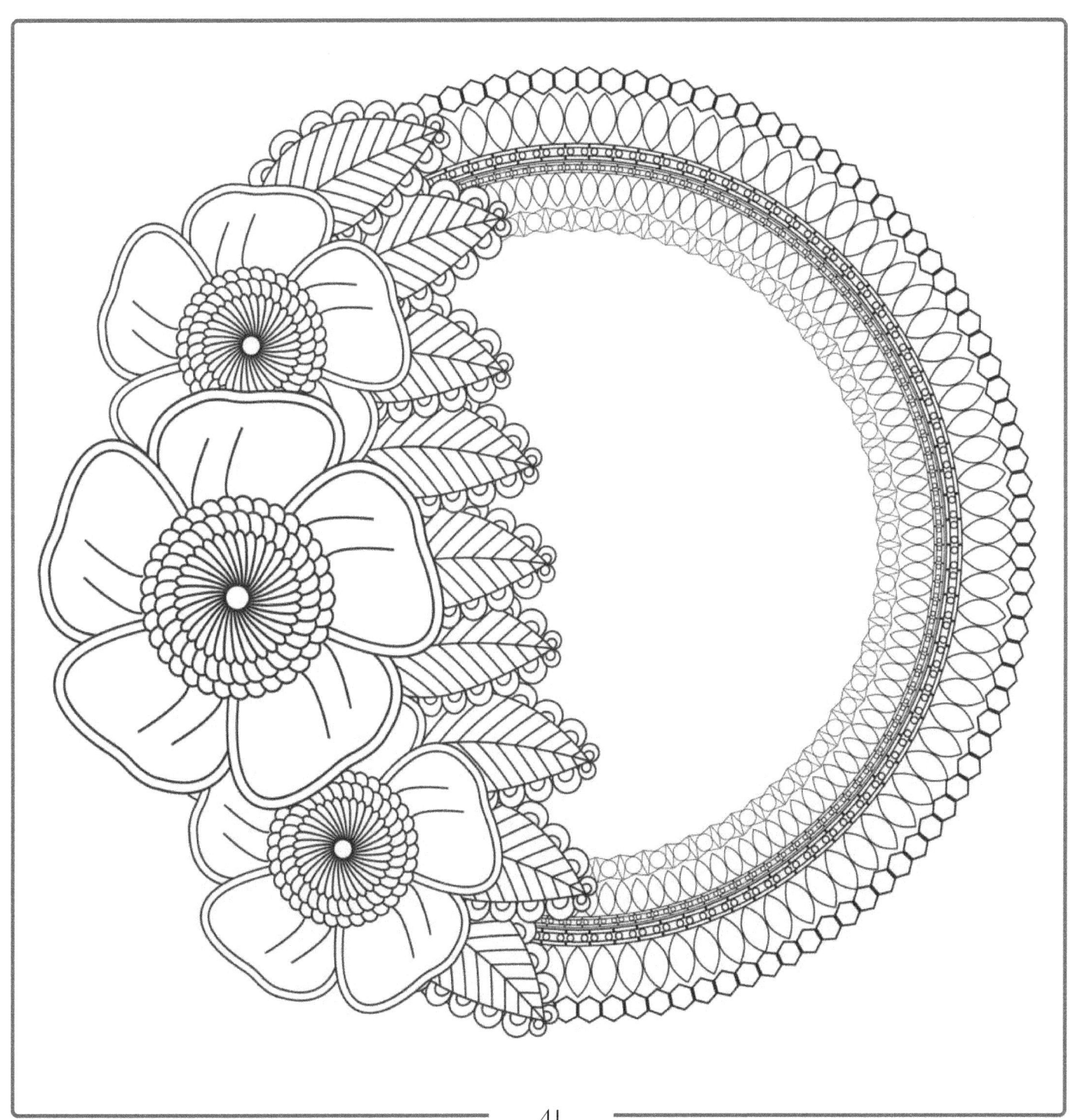

Life has its ups
and downs,
but no one has to
be down
for you to be up.

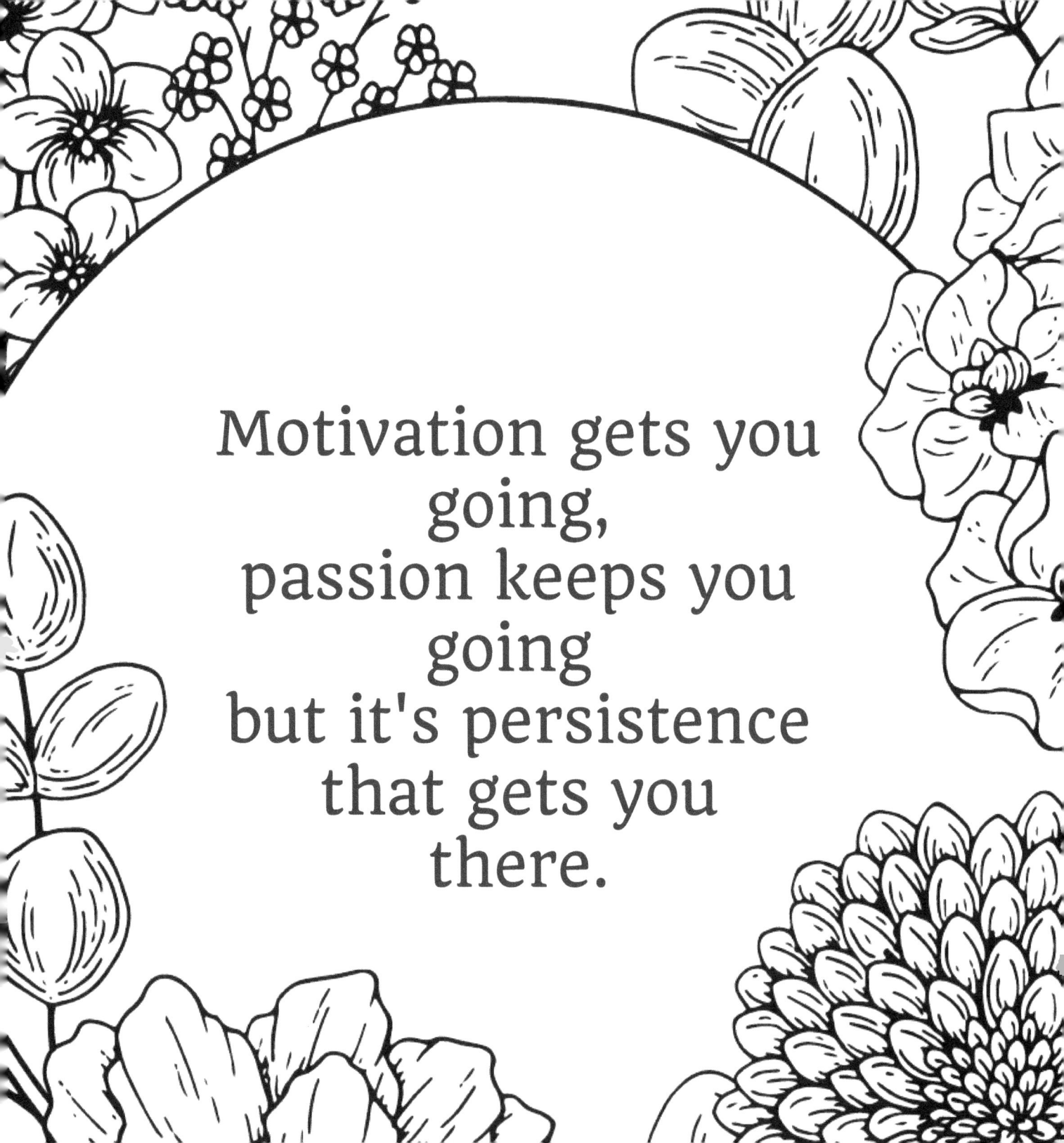

Motivation gets you going,
passion keeps you going
but it's persistence that gets you there.

No amount of powder
can puff away an
ugly character.

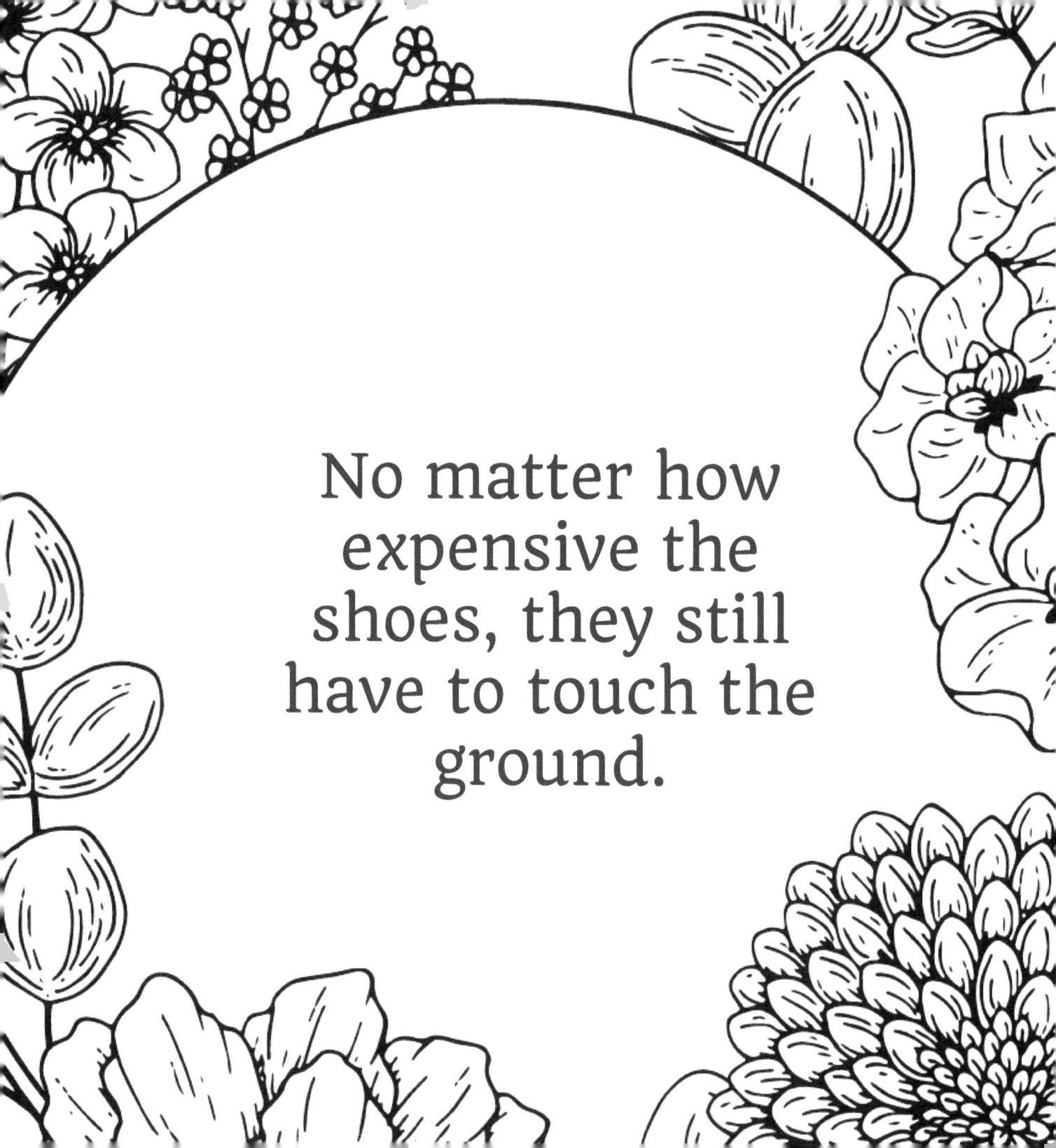

No matter how expensive the shoes, they still have to touch the ground.

No one can know everything,
do everything or be everything;
don't be afraid to ask for help.

Opportunities do not appear for those who don't prepare.

Sometimes it's harder to do nothing.

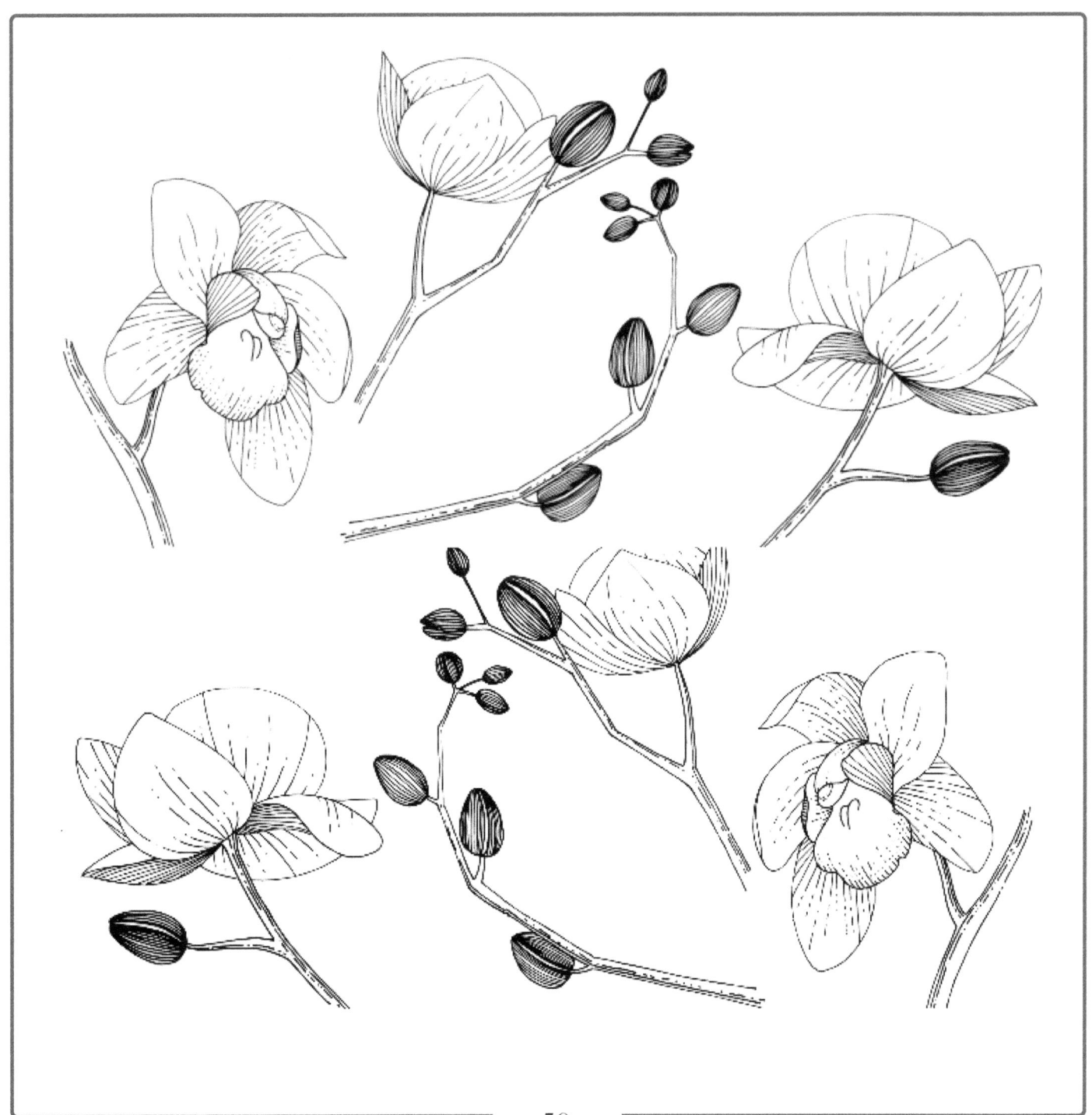

Sometimes the best way to speak to someone is to say nothing.

Sow where you don't expect to reap.

Stepping stones may look like stumbling blocks.

Talent without ambition makes for wasted gifting.

The journey of a thousand miles begins in the mind.

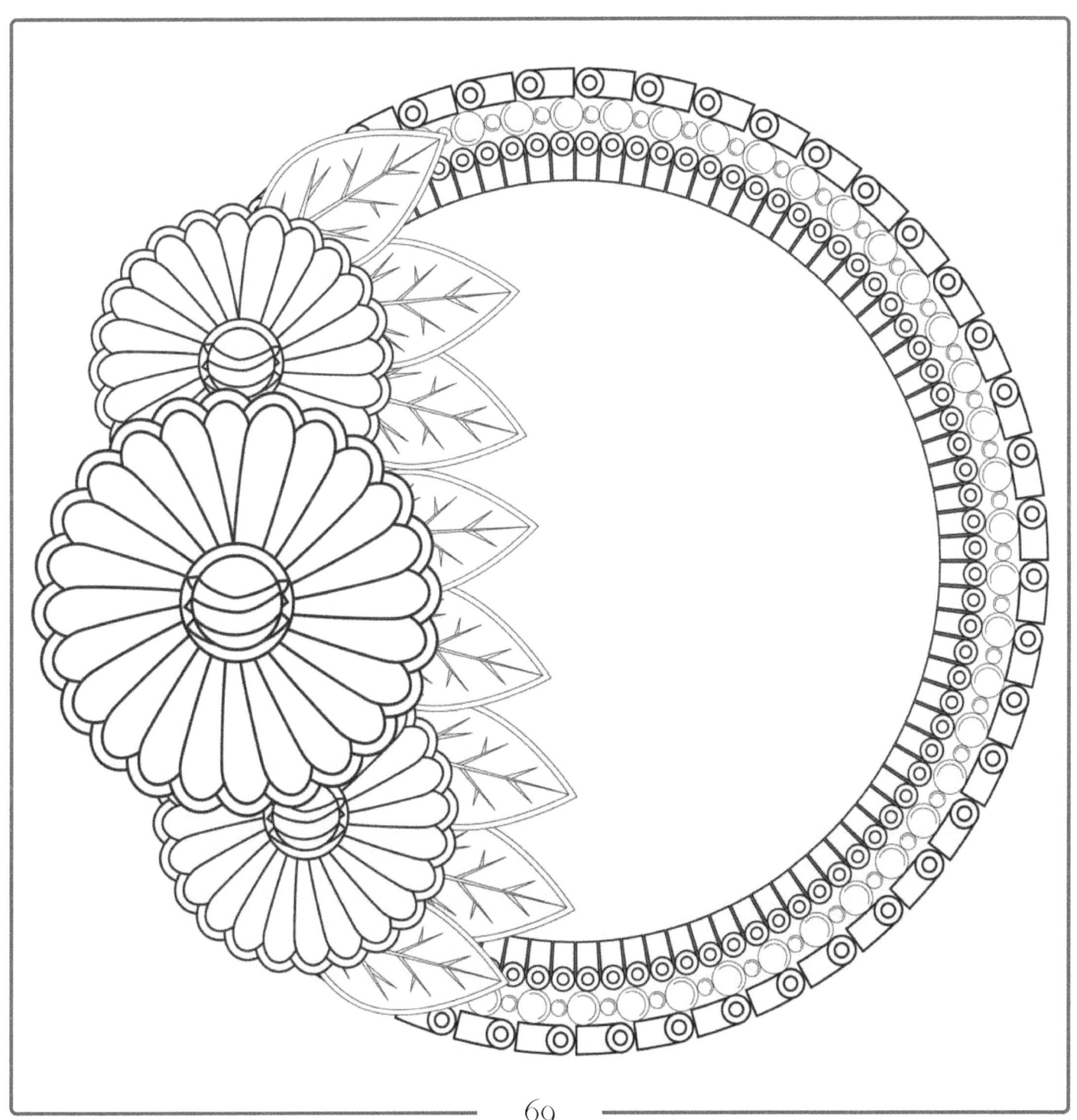

The pain is greater when it's later.

The road to success is dogged by urges to quit. Don't let the dogs out!

Those who have never failed have never tried.

Until you are
willing to take the
first step,
don't think about
the next level.

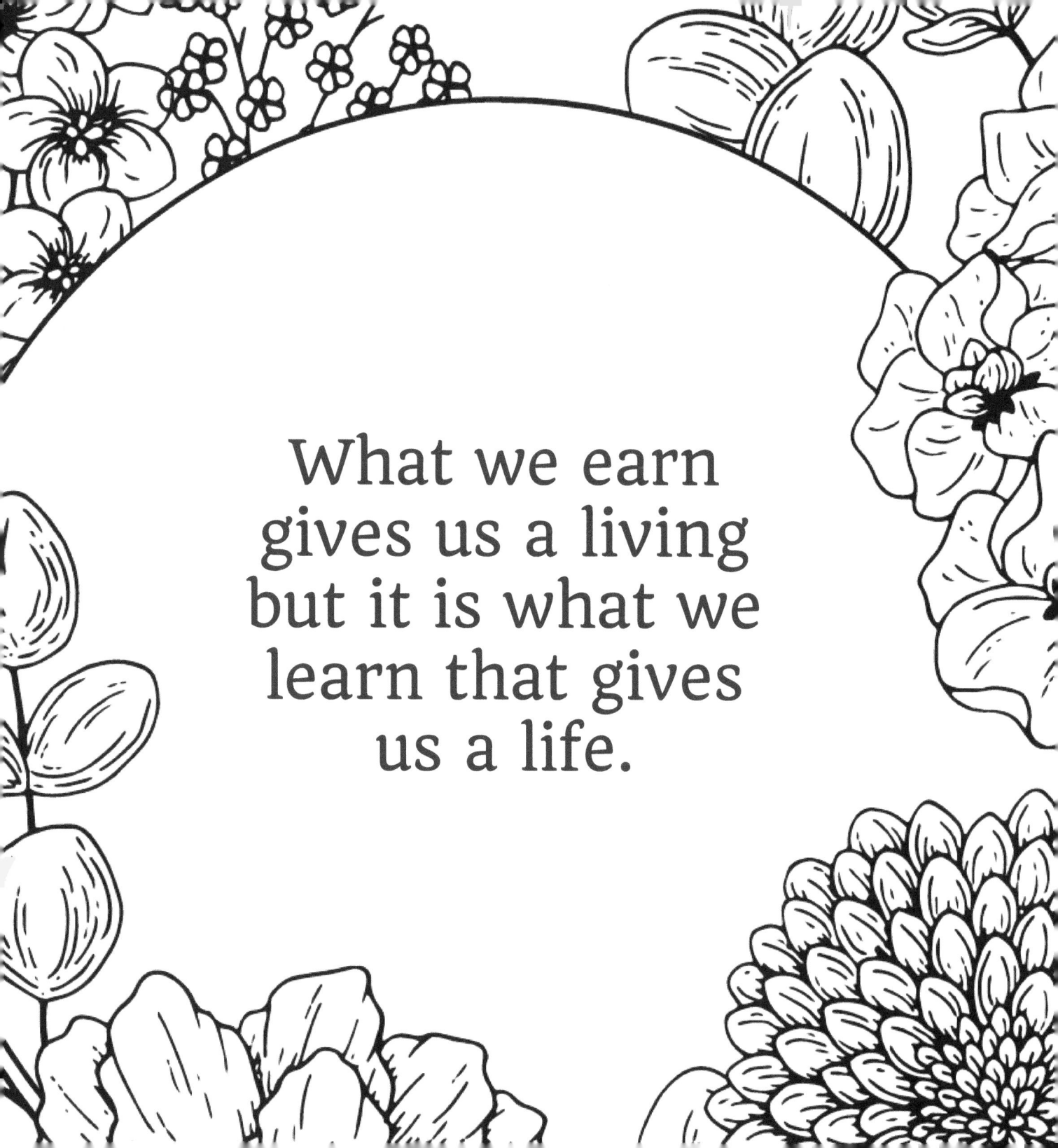

What we earn gives us a living but it is what we learn that gives us a life.

When the ball falls into the gutter,
it's time to get out of the game.

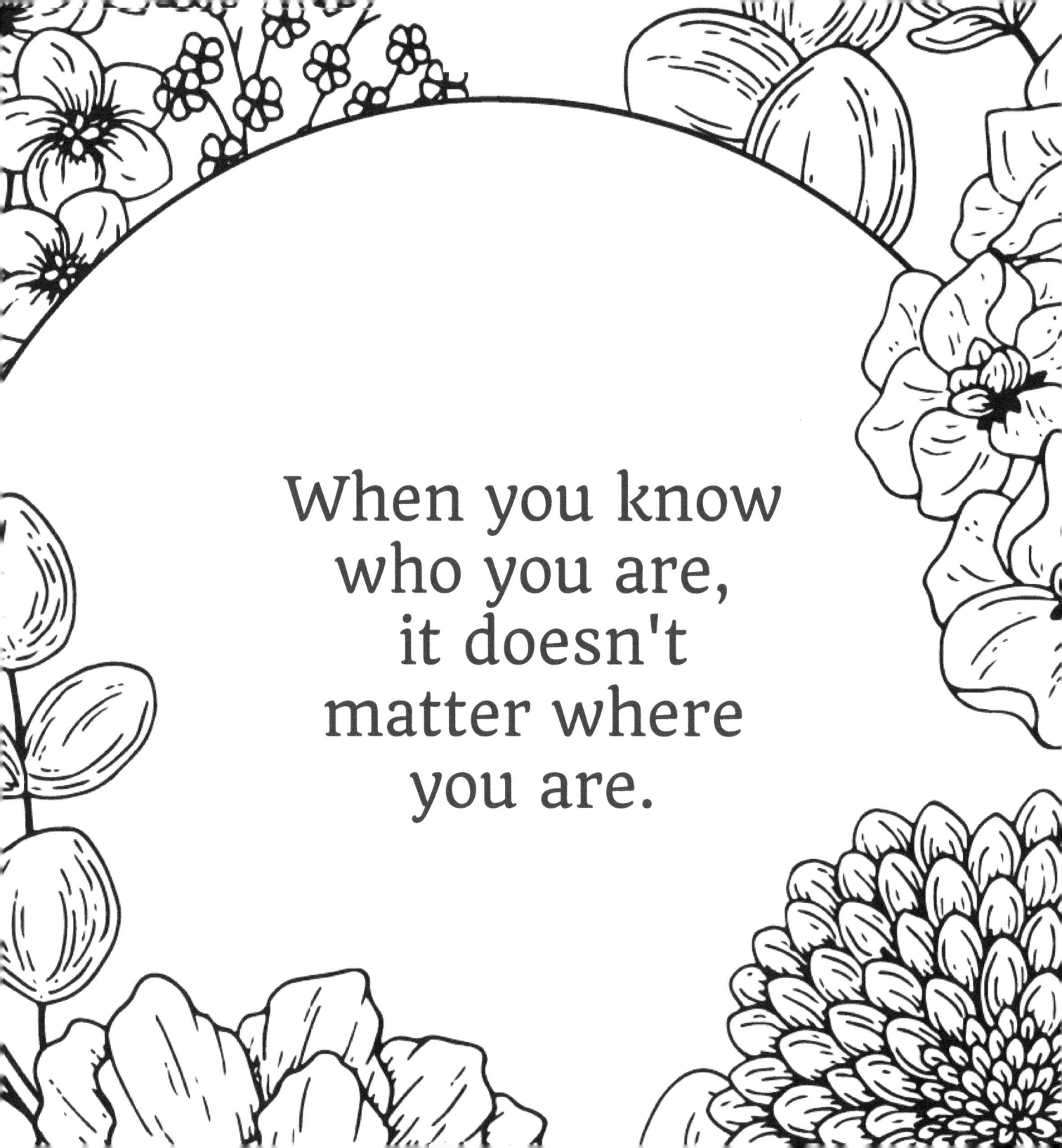

When you know who you are, it doesn't matter where you are.

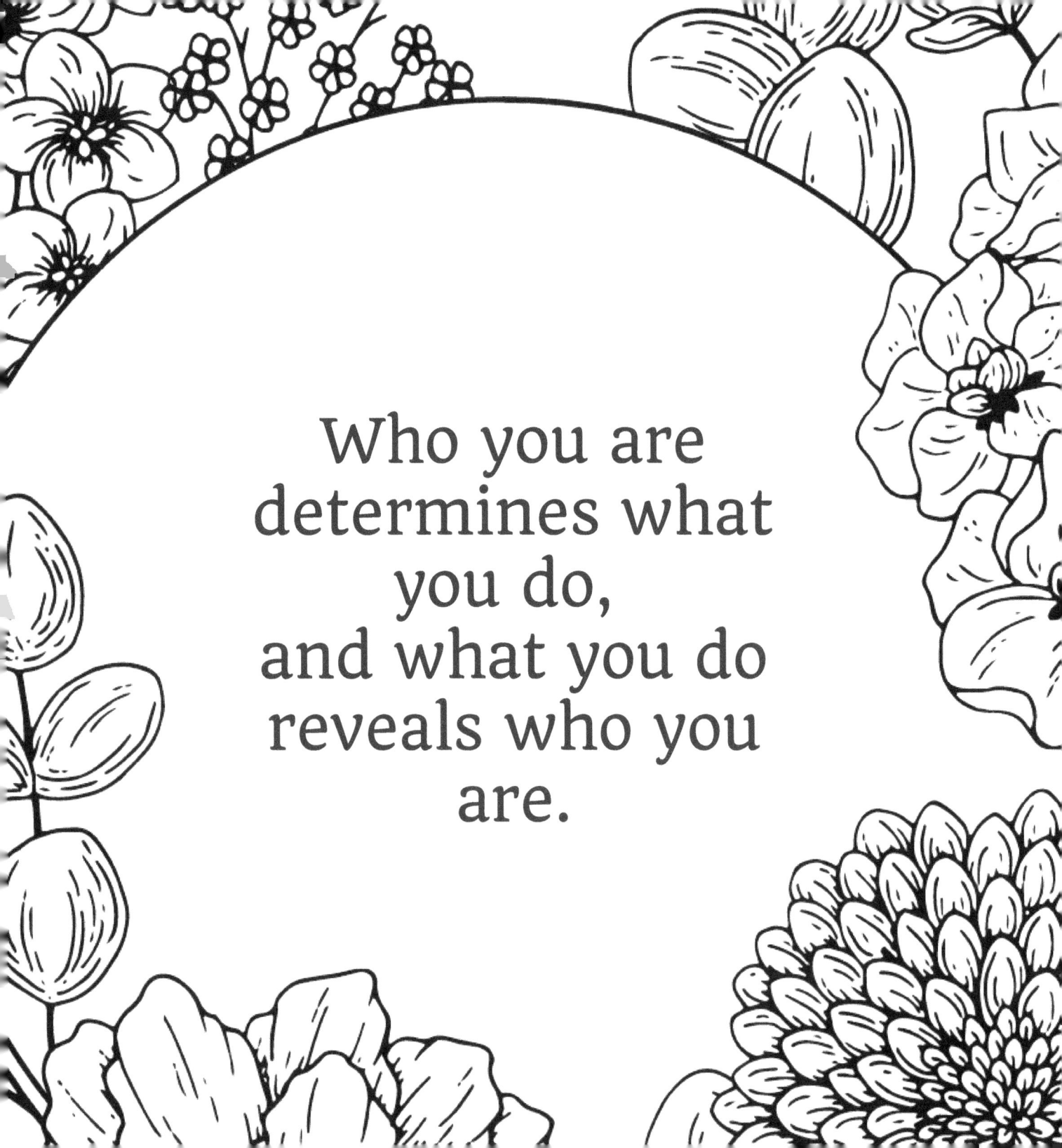

Who you are determines what you do,
and what you do reveals who you are.

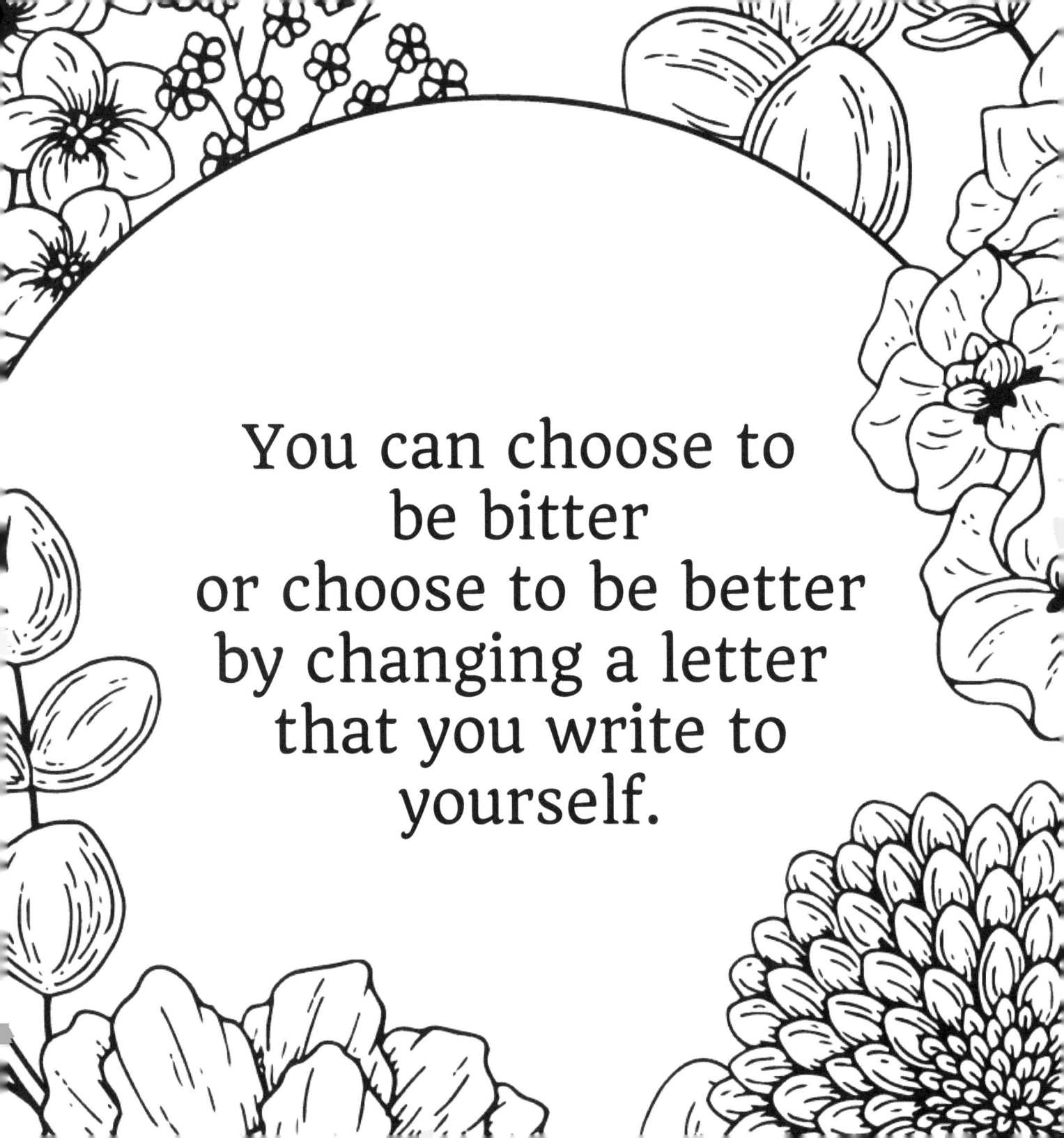

You can choose to
be bitter
or choose to be better
by changing a letter
that you write to
yourself.

You can do a good thing
but it may not be
the right thing.

You can't go places with people who aren't going anywhere.

You can't lock yourself behind a door and then complain that no one is reaching out to you.

You can't sit on it and expect it to move.

Your dream is planted inside you; don't worry if others can't see it or don't share it. Just don't let them stifle it.

Your mentor is not the person who advises you; it's the person whose advice you follow.

www.ingramcontent.com/pod-product-compliance
Lightning Source LLC
Chambersburg PA
CBHW040123130526
44590CB00052B/4486